COUNTRIES OF THE WORLD

Mexico

by Monika Davies

BELLWETHER MEDIA · MINNEAPOLIS, MN

Blastoff! Readers are carefully developed by literacy experts to build reading stamina and move students toward fluency by combining standards-based content with developmentally appropriate text.

 Level 1 provides the most support through repetition of high-frequency words, light text, predictable sentence patterns, and strong visual support.

 Level 2 offers early readers a bit more challenge through varied sentences, increased text load, and text-supportive special features.

 Level 3 advances early-fluent readers toward fluency through increased text load, less reliance on photos, advancing concepts, longer sentences, and more complex special features.

★ **Blastoff! Universe**

Reading Level

Grade
K

Grades
1-3

Grade
4

This edition first published in 2023 by Bellwether Media, Inc.

No part of this publication may be reproduced in whole or in part without written permission of the publisher. For information regarding permission, write to Bellwether Media, Inc., Attention: Permissions Department, 6012 Blue Circle Drive, Minnetonka, MN 55343.

Library of Gongress Cataloging-in-Publication Data

Names: Davies, Monika, author.
Title: Mexico / by Monika Davies.
Description: Minneapolis, MN : Bellwether Media, Inc., 2023. | Series: Blastoff! Readers: countries of the world | Includes bibliographical references and index. | Audience: Ages 5-8 | Audience: Grades 2-3 | Summary: "Relevant images match informative text in this introduction to Mexico. Intended for students in kindergarten through third grade"– Provided by publisher.
Identifiers: LCCN 2022018254 (print) | LCCN 2022018255 (ebook) | ISBN 9781644877234 (library binding) | ISBN 9781648347696 (ebook)
Subjects: LCSH: Mexico–Juvenile literature.
Classification: LCC F1208.5 .D38 2023 (print) | LCC F1208.5 (ebook) | DDC 972–dc23/eng/20220420
LC record available at https://lccn.loc.gov/2022018254
LC ebook record available at https://lccn.loc.gov/2022018255

Editor: Elizabeth Neuenfeldt   Designer: Gabriel Hilger

Printed in the United States of America, North Mankato, MN.

Table of Contents

All About Mexico

Mexico City

Mexico is a country full of life.
Over 100 million people live there!

Mexico is located
in North America.
Its capital is Mexico City.

Mexico City,
Mexico

Land and Animals

A **plateau** covers northern and central Mexico. The Sierra Madres surround it. These mountains are home to **volcanoes**.

Rain forests are in southern Mexico. **Coral reefs** stretch along the east coast.

coral reef

Citlaltépetl Volcano

Size: 18,406 feet (5,610 meters) tall

Famous For: highest mountain
in Mexico

Northern Mexico has hot, dry summers. Winters are cold in the mountains.

Southern Mexico is warm year-round. The rain forests are hot and **humid**.

Mexico is full of wildlife!
Coyotes live in the north.
Monarch butterflies **migrate**
to Mexico each winter.

monarch
butterfly

Animals of Mexico

coyote

jaguar

keel-billed
toucan

green turtle

Jaguars and toucans live
in rain forests. Green turtles
swim through reefs.

Mexicans call Mexico home. Most Mexicans speak Spanish. Many are **Catholics**.

Mexicans mainly live in cities. Some live in the countryside.

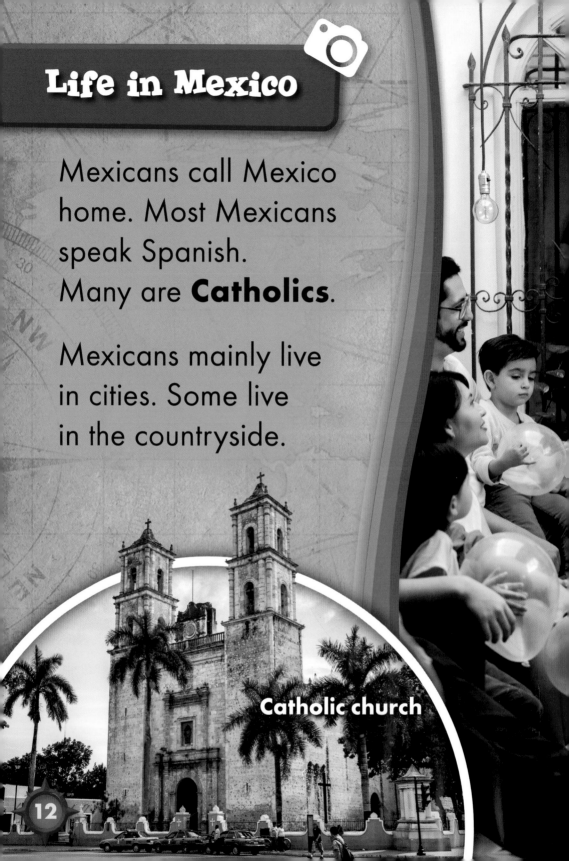

Catholic church

soccer

boxing

Soccer is a top sport in Mexico. Mexicans love cheering for their favorite teams! Boxing is also popular.

Some people also like to hike and visit beaches.

hiking

Chilaquiles is a well-loved breakfast dish in Mexico. *Pozole* is a tasty stew. *Elotes* are made with corn on the cob.

Mexican Foods

chilaquiles

pozole

elotes

dulce de leche

dulce de leche

Dulce de leche is a sweet treat!

Mexico's national holiday is
September 16. Mexicans
wave flags and light fireworks.

Day of the Dead

Day of the Dead is in November. Families honor **ancestors** with food and flowers. Holidays bring Mexicans together!

Mexico Facts

Size:
758,449 square miles
(1,964,375 square kilometers)

Population:
129,150,971 (2022)

National Holiday:
Independence Day (September 16)

Main Language:
Spanish

Capital City:
Mexico City

Famous Face

Name: Frida Kahlo

Famous For: an artist known
for her paintings

Religions

Roman Catholic: 78%

other Christian: 11%

other or none: 11%

Top Landmarks

Chichén Itzá

Monte Albán

Tulum

Glossary

ancestors—relatives who lived long ago

Catholics—people belonging to the Roman Catholic Church

coral reefs—groups of corals that grow in warm, shallow ocean waters

humid—having a lot of water in the air

migrate—to move from one place to another, often with the seasons

plateau—a flat, raised area of land

rain forests—thick, green forests that receive a lot of rain

volcanoes—holes in the earth; when a volcano erupts, hot ash, gas, or melted rock called lava shoots out.

To Learn More

AT THE LIBRARY

Dean, Jessica. *Mexico*. Minneapolis, Minn.: Pogo, 2019.

Orgullo, Marisa. *Celebrating Day of the Dead!* New York, N.Y.: PowerKids Press, 2019.

Reynolds, A.M. *Let's Look at Mexico*. North Mankato, Minn.: Capstone Press, 2019.

ON THE WEB

FACTSURFER

Factsurfer.com gives you a safe, fun way to find more information.

1. Go to www.factsurfer.com.

2. Enter "Mexico" into the search box and click 🔍.

3. Select your book cover to see a list of related content.

Index